W9-AAJ-490

CONTEMPORARY MUSICIANS
AND THEIR MUSIC™

LINKIN PARK

Greg Saulmon

The Rosen Publishing Group, Inc., New York

For Pete Sorbi, who inspired me to start playing music and writing

Published in 2007 by The Rosen Publishing Group, Inc.
29 East 21st Street, New York, NY 10010

Library of Congress Cataloging-in-Publication Data

Saulmon, Greg.
Linkin Park/by Greg Saulmon.—1st ed.
    p. cm.—(Contemporary musicians and their music)
Includes discography (p.   ), bibliographical references (p.   ), and index.
ISBN 1-4042-0713-9 (library binding)
1. Linkin Park (Musical group)—Juvenile literature. 2. Rock musicians—United States—Biography—Juvenile literature.
I. Title. II. Series.
ML3930.L56S38 2007
782.42166092'2aB—dc22

                                                    2005033390

On the cover: Joe Hahn, Mike Shinoda, Rob Bourdon, Dave Farrell, Brad Delson, and Chester Bennington *(from left)* are the members of Linkin Park.

Contents

Introduction

Stepping onto a stage in Malaysia must have been one of the strangest experiences of Chester Bennington's life. There were the obvious reasons. The Malaysian government, in response to concerns from the country's vast Muslim population, had set strict guidelines for the show. The band members would not be allowed to wear shorts or spit on stage. They would not be allowed to swear or jump around during the performance.

It was a far cry from the anything-goes mind-set ruling most American concerts. But Linkin Park had

Chester Bennington (center), Joe Hahn (back), and Dave Farrell (right) work the stage with Jay-Z in Malaysia.

no trouble following the rules. The members were there for their fans. They didn't want anyone to go home disappointed because the concert was cut short.

Still, there were other reasons for Bennington to feel strange. Fewer than ten years before, he'd been just another troubled kid on the streets of Phoenix, Arizona. He was addicted to drugs, working at a fast-food restaurant, and probably headed nowhere.

Now, here he was on the other side of the world. He was performing for a sold-out crowd of 50,000—a crowd more than twice as large as the population of the towns where some of his bandmates had grown up.

It was one of the biggest shows of Linkin Park's fairly short but more than impressive career. The band's albums had sold millions upon millions of copies. The band walked home with a Grammy Award after releasing just one album. It had toured with some of the biggest names in the music business. Now Linkin Park was one of the biggest names. And it had won fans all around the world.

For Bennington and the other members of Linkin Park, they were living a dream they'd been working toward since high school.

Chapter One

Rock and Roll High School

Rob Bourdon got an early start in music. After a close-up look at Joey Kramer's drum-playing during an Aerosmith concert, Bourdon decided to take up the instrument. He began pounding the skins when he was just ten.

Bourdon attended Agoura High School in the Los Angeles, California, suburb of Agoura Hills. There, he met a purple-haired guitarist (and former trumpet player) named Brad Delson. The two formed a band called Relative Degree. They set a goal of playing a show at the Roxy, a famous club in West Hollywood. They wrote twelve songs, practiced them for a year, and finally landed a gig at the Roxy. After having reached its goal, Relative Degree broke up.

Drummer Rob Bourdon's first performance was at a party when he was in the sixth grade. Aerosmith drummer Joey Kramer, who was a friend of Bourdon's mother's, inspired the young Bourdon to try drums.

The show at the Roxy, as fate would have it, wasn't the most important musical moment for the members of Relative Degree. Another classmate, a rapper named Mike Shinoda, sometimes hung out at Relative Degree rehearsals. He and Delson had been friends since middle school, but in terms of music they seemed miles apart. Shinoda was a huge fan of acts such as Run-D.M.C., the Beastie Boys, LL Cool J, and Boogie Down Productions. His interest in rap and hip-hop, which he indulged by creating beats for local MCs, seemed to clash with Delson's hard rock and punk influences.

Despite Delson's and Shinoda's different tastes, they wanted to see how their styles would blend together and where working together would take them. "One of the first songs we wrote, we were like, 'Let's try to collide these different styles of music,'"

Guitarist Brad Delson *(left)* rocks out in his trademark headphones while Bourdon (on drums) and Farrell *(right)* add their own intensity. Delson's headphones are custom made. He's rarely seen without them onstage.

Delson told MTV. "It really was somewhat crude at that point, because you could hear, 'OK, here's the hip-hop verse and here's the rock chorus.'" The two kept at it, piecing together tracks in Delson's bedroom studio.

Coming Together at College

Shinoda and Delson spent several months writing songs. Soon, they were ready to try them out with a full band. Although they went to different colleges, they kept in touch with each other and with Bourdon. At college, they found the people they needed to make their music come to life.

Shinoda's interest in art took him to the Art Center College of Design in Pasadena, California. He studied illustration by day and worked on his music by night. He met Joe Hahn, a DJ, at the school. At UCLA—where Delson eventually earned a bachelor's degree in communications—he shared an apartment with a bass player named Dave "Phoenix" Farrell. With all the instruments in place, Shinoda, Delson, Bourdon, Farrell, and Hahn teamed up with vocalist Mark Wakefield to form a band called Super Xero. The group eventually renamed itself Xero and began recording a demo.

Like many would-be stars, though, Xero failed to generate much interest. It began to look like the band would break up. Wakefield quit. Farrell finished college and ended up touring with a band called the Snax for almost a year and a half. (He didn't reunite with Shinoda and company until his old friends had resurfaced as Linkin Park and were about to release an album called *Hybrid Theory*.) Delson was committed to the music, but he also made plans to go to law school.

Still, Shinoda was determined to make it. Xero had made a few contacts in the record industry. He was convinced that they

LINKIN PARK AT A GLANCE

Brad Delson *(left)*
Instrument: Guitar
Hometown: Agoura Hills, California

Joe Hahn ("Mr. Hahn," "Remy")
 (second from left)
Instruments: Turntables
Hometown: Glendale, California

Chester Bennington *(third from left)*
Instrument: Vocals
Hometown: Phoenix, Arizona

Rob Bourdon *(third from right)*
Instrument: Drums
Hometown: Calabasas, California

Mike Shinoda *(second from right)*
Instruments: Vocals, keyboards, and guitar
Hometown: Agoura Hills, California

Dave Farrell ("Phoenix") *(right)*
Instrument: Bass
Hometown: Plymouth, Massachusetts

were just missing one piece that would set them on the track to fame. Shinoda began looking for a vocalist.

Enter Bennington

Hundreds of miles away, a singer named Chester Bennington had been making noise in Phoenix, Arizona. His band, Grey Daze, built a decent following after forming in 1993. The band recorded two albums, *No Sun Today* and *Wake Me*. The band even contacted an attorney in Los Angeles to help present its music to major labels.

Performing music was a goal Bennington had been working toward for as long as he could remember. Even as a toddler he seemed to have rock-star dreams. His older brother, Brian, introduced him to classic rock bands such as Foreigner and Rush. Little Chester sang Depeche Mode songs around the house (Linkin Park still cites the band as a major influence). He started listening to hip-hop acts such as the Sugar Hill Gang and Slick Rick during middle school.

His life changed when he saw a Stone Temple Pilots concert at the age of fourteen. Frontman Scott Weiland (now the singer for Velvet Revolver) inspired Bennington. Although Bennington's first instrument had been piano, Weiland's huge stage presence

Chester Bennington's amazing vocal talents wowed the members of Xero (the band that later became Linkin Park) during his audition, as did his lifelong passion for music.

and jaw-dropping vocals made Bennington realize what he really wanted to do: sing. He formed his first band, Sean Dowdell and His Friends, early on in high school. (The band's namesake, Sean Dowdell, went on to be one of Bennington's bandmates in Grey Daze.) Bennington was the lead singer. He worked on his vocals constantly.

Music was one of his only positive escapes. Bennington's childhood hadn't been easy. His family moved often. He lived all over Arizona, including Scottsdale, Tolleson, Tempe, and Phoenix. Then, his parents divorced when he was eleven. Bennington went to live with his father, a police detective. In order to deal with the pain of his parents' divorce—and, even worse, with the fact that someone outside his family had sexually abused him—Bennington began smoking pot. His schoolwork started to suffer. He lost interest in the sports at which he'd always been good.

High school didn't bring any better luck. One of Bennington's close friends committed suicide, and another died in a skateboarding accident. He began to experiment with other drugs, such as alcohol, LSD, and methamphetamines.

By the time he graduated from high school, Bennington was addicted to cocaine and crystal meth. These are powerful, dangerous drugs that have ruined many people's lives. Luckily, he found a savior. In 1996, he was working part-time at a fast-food restaurant. It didn't pay much, but it gave him the time to spend all night practicing music. One day, Bennington met a woman named Samantha.

She happened to be a Grey Daze fan. He fell in love with her, but he was worried he didn't have much to offer. He slept on a futon and rode his skateboard to work—he couldn't afford a bike, much less a car. But he was devoted to his music, and she understood. The couple began dating and got married on Halloween that year.

Linking Up

Samantha was the best thing that had ever happened to Bennington. He credits her (along

When Bennington first met his wife, Samantha, he wasn't just a drug addict—he was also very poor. After they married, Bennington turned his life around. He and Samantha eventually owned two homes in Arizona.

with his mother, a nurse) with helping him kick his drug habit. She also offered the emotional support he needed to deal with the painful memories of his childhood.

He and Samantha continued to live in the Phoenix area. Samantha was working in real estate, and Bennington was sneaking into business classes at a local college. Unlike his future bandmates, Bennington never earned a college degree.

Grey Daze had broken up, and Bennington was looking for a new musical outlet. That's when luck struck. The attorney who had worked with Grey Daze contacted Bennington. He'd been working with a band called Xero that was looking for a singer.

Bennington contacted the band to set up an audition. Xero sent a demo of its songs, and Bennington was told to prepare vocals. After receiving the tape on a Saturday morning, Bennington went to a professional studio that night to record. He called Mike Shinoda on Sunday and played the tape over the phone. Shinoda was floored. He asked whether Bennington could come to Los Angeles immediately.

It was the chance of a lifetime. Bennington went to Los Angeles for his official audition. It went well, so Xero started rehearsing with Bennington while conducting the remaining auditions. But even Bennington's competitors knew Xero had already found the perfect fit. Bennington recalled to MTV, "One guy came in a couple of songs before our practice was over. He was sitting there and they were like, 'OK, you ready?' He stood up and said, 'You know what, I'm going to leave.' And they were like, 'Why? What's going on?' He's like, 'If you're not gonna take this guy, you're stupid.' And he just left. That was kind of the last audition."

Bennington made the difficult decision to leave Samantha in Phoenix to try his shot at stardom. She knew he was following a lifelong dream, so she bravely stayed behind to pay their bills. Bennington promised that they'd be together again as soon as he figured out whether Xero would find fame or failure. It wouldn't be long before his question was answered.

Chapter Two

The Fame Game

Bennington's leap of faith was a shot in the arm for the members of Xero. They knew Bennington was serious, and they prepared to work hard for their shot at the big time. Bennington and Shinoda started to collaborate on lyrics, and the band began exploring new musical ideas.

As the band created its identity, the members began searching for a new name. The group rejected Clear, Probing Lagers, Ten PM Stocker, and Platinum Lotus Foundation before finally settling on Hybrid Theory. Bennington had suggested the name because he thought it was an accurate description of the music—a "hybrid" of rock and rap. The name was the final piece of the puzzle. Hybrid Theory was ready to hit the stage.

Bennington poses with vocalist Mike Shinoda *(right)* at the premier of *The Matrix Reloaded*. Linkin Park contributed the song "Session" to the movie's soundtrack, which also includes songs by Rob Zombie; Marilyn Manson; and the Dave Matthews Band, a favorite of Linkin Park drummer Rob Bourdon.

Record Labels Take Notice

Hybrid Theory played its first show at a Los Angeles club called the Whisky a Go Go. In the audience was Jeff Blue, a representative from Zomba Music Publishing (guitarist Delson had interned at Zomba). The band's scorching set made quite an impression on Blue. That very night, he offered a publishing deal. The deal gave the band the money it needed to record a CD that it could use to court major labels and sell at shows.

After selling a handful of copies of the Hybrid Theory EP, the band decided to harness the power of the Internet. The members started seeking fans online, talking themselves up in chat rooms, and sending free copies of the CD—along with stickers and other free merchandise—to anyone who seemed interested. Online fans around the country eventually formed an informal "street team" that helped Hybrid Theory spread its music.

Even though its fan base was growing, it was still striking out with major labels. Hybrid Theory played showcase after showcase (almost forty in all) for record executives, only to be rejected each time. At one point, Shinoda was both taking his last set of final exams and performing showcases for six well-known record labels. It was grueling. But the bandmates knew that, if they kept at it, their music would eventually find its way into the right hands.

Those hands happened to belong to executives at the Warner Music Group, one of the world's largest record labels. Warner knew about Hybrid Theory's hard work and dedication to its art. The executives knew the band could be a good investment—especially after several meetings with the band members. Bennington, Shinoda, and company frequently visited Warner's offices to explain their promotional strategies and show evidence from the street team of the band's popularity.

Shinoda, Delson, Bourdon, and Bennington *(back, from left)* push Farrell and Hahn in shopping carts. Riding in shopping carts is probably about as comfortable as the tiny van Linkin Park used for its early tours. Back then, the members had to load their own gear into and out of clubs, night after night.

It took years of hard work and dedication. The band's members had to juggle school and work while pursuing their passion. By spring 2000, their perseverance paid off. Hybrid Theory had landed a recording contract with Warner.

A Park Called Lincoln

It wasn't long before Hybrid Theory hit a roadblock. A band called Hybrid had emerged on the L.A. scene. Seeking to avoid confusing fans (and the possibility of a legal dispute), Bennington and his bandmates went back to the drawing board.

It hit Bennington on the way home from rehearsal one night. His commute took him past a place in Santa Monica, California, called Lincoln Park. He thought the name sounded catchy, so he suggested it to the band. The other members agreed. It had an energy and power to it.

There was just one problem with Bennington's idea. A Web site (http://www.lincolnpark.com) already existed, and the band didn't have enough money to buy the domain name. Bennington and the others realized the importance of the Internet as a tool for promoting their music. After all, it was the online community of fans that had been a major factor in their success so far. As Shinoda explained to Yahoo! Music, "We wanted our own website, 'cause our main channel to talk to our fans was on the Web; we're very active on the Web . . . Now we have our message boards and our chat rooms . . . we can talk to our fans directly online."

In the end, the solution was simple. The band started thinking about using a different spelling of "Lincoln Park." When the members discovered that http://www.linkinpark.com was available, they knew they had a name that worked.

The band quickly learned that it was a good choice. Brad Delson told *Guitar World*, "We went on tour right after we changed the name, and we pretty quickly realized there was a Lincoln Park in every town. Kids would come up to us and go, 'Dude! You're from Lincoln Park too? What side?' The joke, basically, is that everywhere we go, people think we're local. So in that respect, it's a really cool name."

Since that fateful name change, Linkin Park's namesake has had a change of its own. Lincoln Park in Santa Monica, California, has been renamed Christine Emerson Reed Park, after a former city council member.

The Album Drops

Linkin Park had every reason to be optimistic. The response to the music at shows and online was overwhelmingly positive. Moreover, the Warner deal would allow the band to release its first full-length album. But scoring a deal with a major label doesn't always guarantee fame and fortune. For every band that goes on to superstardom, there are dozens of others that, despite great expectations, fail to find an audience.

Putting out an album is no easy task. Along with all of the work that goes into songwriting, there are literally hundreds and hundreds of decisions that need to be made. The band must decide how each instrument should sound (even how each individual drum should sound), which samples should go where, and the order in which the songs will appear. Not to mention the decisions outside the music, such as what the album art will look like. Through the whole process, there were questions that were hard to ignore: What if it's not good enough? What if nobody buys it? But Linkin Park tried to keep things in perspective. The members focused on putting out an album with which they were happy. They knew that, if they stayed true to their music, the rest would fall into place.

Linkin Park's album *Hybrid Theory* hit the stores in fall 2000, and people did buy it. A lot of people, in fact. The album debuted at number 16 on Billboard's Top 200 albums chart. It was a nearly unprecedented feat for a relatively unknown band. The success of *Hybrid Theory* quickly took on epic proportions. It became the best-selling album of 2001. In December 2002, well over a year after its release, it remained the fifth best-selling album on the charts. Linkin Park had arrived.

The fans weren't the only ones who were impressed. Critics were taking notice, too. In January 2002, Linkin Park received three Grammy nominations. At the star-studded awards ceremony, Bennington, Shinoda, Delson, Bourdon, Hahn, and Farrell walked away with a Grammy Award for Best Hard Rock Performance for the song "Crawling." For many musicians, winning a Grammy is a lifelong dream, and Linkin Park members were no exceptions. "Certainly winning a Grammy for me was huge," Delson told

ROAD WARRIORS

One of Linkin Park's first major tours was Ozzfest 2001. Organized by the legendary Ozzy Osbourne, each year's Ozzfest tour features some of the biggest names in heavy metal. Linkin Park played alongside bands such as Marilyn Manson, Slipknot, Papa Roach, and Disturbed. The band members toured in a bus outfitted with a recording studio. The comfort was especially welcomed, considering that Linkin Park played 324 shows in 2001.

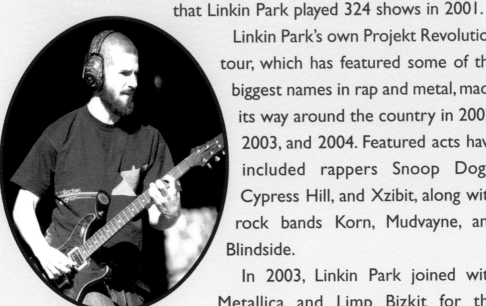

Brad Delson at the Summer Sanitarium Tour 2003

Linkin Park's own Projekt Revolution tour, which has featured some of the biggest names in rap and metal, made its way around the country in 2002, 2003, and 2004. Featured acts have included rappers Snoop Dogg, Cypress Hill, and Xzibit, along with rock bands Korn, Mudvayne, and Blindside.

In 2003, Linkin Park joined with Metallica and Limp Bizkit for the Summer Sanitarium tour. Performances in Dallas and Houston from this tour appear on the band's CD/DVD set, *Live in Texas*. The year 2004 brought Linkin Park's biggest tour yet. Supporting its new album, the band launched the Meteora World Tour with openers P.O.D., Hoobastank, and Story of the Year.

Farrell, Hahn, Bennington, Bourdon, Delson, and Shinoda *(from left)* show off the Grammy Linkin Park won for the song "Crawling." In 2002, the band was nominated in the categories Best New Artist, Best Rock Album, and Best Hard Rock Performance.

Yahoo! Music. "Mike actually, that was one of his goals, to win a Grammy, and we all looked at him like he was crazy. Then when we won one, we were ecstatic."

Over the next few years, Linkin Park's distinctive style continued to win fans the world over, bringing the band to levels of success the six bandmates never dreamed they'd reach.

Chapter Three

Behind the Music

By the mid- to late 1990s, the grunge movement that had dominated the airwaves seemed to be drawing to a close. Kurt Cobain's suicide in 1994 ended the career of Nirvana, one of the genre's most successful bands. Other acts, such as Pearl Jam, Smashing Pumpkins, and Soundgarden, either broke up or began to fade from the public eye. But the influence of heavy metal and punk could still be heard in the new generation of bands that were gaining popularity.

Bands such as Korn and the Deftones featured the loud, aggressive guitars and vocals that had always characterized metal. But they mixed these sounds with drumbeats that often had a hip-hop influence. They also made frequent use of samples and other elements of electronic music. Bands like Rage Against the Machine and eventually Limp Bizkit combined traditional rock instruments and riffs with rap-influenced vocals. As more and more bands emerged, it appeared that a new genre was taking shape. People started looking for a way to label it. Many began referring to it as new metal or nü-metal.

Linkin Park has often been called a nü-metal band. Its members, though, are less than pleased with the label. Shinoda said in an interview with the software company Native Instruments, "We don't care much for the whole 'new metal' thing. We just make music that we want to listen to. Rather than writing to be part of a genre, we just write what we feel moved by."

A Sound of Their Own

The marriage of rock and rap can be traced back to at least the 1980s. The collaboration of Aerosmith and Run-D.M.C. on the song "Walk This Way" is one of the earliest examples. Around the same time, the Beastie Boys were rapping over rock guitars on songs such as "No Sleep Till Brooklyn" and "Fight for Your Right to Party." The year 1991 saw metal band Anthrax team up with rap legends Public Enemy on the raging track "Bring Tha Noize." (Not surprising, Shinoda cites seeing Anthrax and Public

The original members of Depeche Mode were *(from left)* Martin Gore, Andy Fletcher, Dave Gahan, and Alan Wilder. Linkin Park cites this 1980s pop band as an influence on its own music. Mike Shinoda remixed Depeche Mode's classic "Enjoy the Silence" for a single in 2004.

Enemy in concert as one of his major inspirations.)

But Linkin Park's influences include more than just the rap/rock collaborations that came before it. When asked about their influences, band members often mention rap groups such as the Roots, "industrial" metal bands such as Nine Inch Nails, pop groups such as Depeche Mode, and electronic groups such as Aphex Twin. Linkin Park draws inspiration and ideas from this deep pool of music to create its own innovative style.

A typical Linkin Park song (if there is such a thing) is a burst of energy that takes the listener on an emotional roller coaster. Heavy guitar riffs play off more subdued instrumental sections featuring keyboards or even Japanese flutes. Shinoda weaves his smooth flow in and out of Bennington's sometimes soaring, sometimes quiet, and sometimes furious and frenetic vocals.

Their sound is not always easy to describe, and the band prefers it that way. "By talking about it, we're just promoting it," Shinoda told British newspaper the *Guardian*. "If you really want to know what the band's about, listen to the CD or come to the show or visit the Web site. You can't expect to know what we're about by reading about us in a magazine."

HEAVY SOUNDS, MELLOW TASTE

It's often surprising to learn what people who play loud music listen to in their spare time. For example, Ozzy Osbourne is a devoted fan of the Beatles. Chino Moreno from the Deftones cites the Cure's singer, Robert Smith, as one of his biggest influences.

The same is true of the members of Linkin Park. "I listen to a lot mellower stuff, like Pete Yorn," drummer Rob Bourdon told Yahoo! Music. "I like the Dave Matthews Band, John Mayer, that kind of stuff. After being on the road with so many other heavy bands and listening to heavier music, sometimes it's nice to listen to Coldplay and chill."

Guitarist Brad Delson is a closet fan of Britney Spears, and Bennington is self-admittedly mad about Madonna's music. Shinoda's first musical outlet wasn't rap or metal—it was classical piano. He took lessons for twelve years.

Songwriting 101

Bands take many different approaches to writing songs. In some bands, a single member comes up with words and music to present to the group as a whole. In other bands, the members work as a group from beginning to end.

Over the years, Linkin Park has developed its own strategy. A song usually begins with two or three members getting together to share ideas. Shinoda is often involved early on, since he's the band "expert" on Pro Tools (a popular software program for recording music). Once an initial idea gets recorded, the other members start suggesting guitar riffs, drum breaks, samples, and other elements.

The song "Somewhere I Belong" is a good example of the way Linkin Park writes songs. It began with an acoustic guitar riff that Shinoda and Hahn turned into a "sample." Imagine a jigsaw puzzle with pieces that, instead of having only one solution, can be put together to create different pictures. That's how samples work—they're bits of music that can be put together in many different ways. They used the software to play Bennington's riff backward and then "cut" it into several different sections. After rearranging the sections to create a new sound, they had the sample that formed the basis of the song.

Bennington performs at Ozzfest in Pittsburgh, Pennsylvania, in July 2001. Ozzfest is a yearly music tour that Ozzy Osbourne and his wife, Sharon, began in 1996.

"Somewhere I Belong" shows how technology plays a major role in the band's songwriting process. The Pro Tools computer program enables a band to change sounds, edit songs, and create high-quality recordings. Best of all, it allows bands to create makeshift studios in sometimes unlikely spaces. Linkin Park recorded early versions of songs from the album *Meteora* in a studio on a tour bus.

The members of Linkin Park are also perfectionists when it comes to recording. They started out with more than fifty song ideas for *Meteora*. They kept narrowing the songs down, keeping only the best ones, until they arrived at the final twelve. As Delson explained to Yahoo! Music, "When we were writing, we definitely wanted to have twelve or thirteen songs that relate to one another, and also sequence them in a way that takes the listener on a journey—not just within each song, but from the beginning of the album to the end."

Linkin's Lyrics

While Linkin Park's music often ends up being a full-band effort, Shinoda and Bennington are responsible for the lyrics. Other members chip in only when they feel the lyrics could use improvement. Bennington recalls rewriting the chorus to "Somewhere I Belong" forty times before the band was happy.

Like many writers, the duo looks for inspiration in personal experiences. Bennington's difficult childhood is a common starting point. But Shinoda and Bennington take a different approach than many "confessional" songwriters. Instead of talking about specific experiences, the pair intentionally keeps the listener guessing. The two songwriters try to be vague, using their lyrics to convey universal emotions to which any listener can relate. For example, the chorus of "In the End" conveys a sense of frustration and hopelessness, but the source of that unhappiness isn't mentioned in the song. This allows the listener to bring his or her own experiences to the song. Someone might have these feelings after a breakup with a girlfriend. Someone else might feel this way because she is having trouble in school.

This strategy is also important because it helps Shinoda and Bennington feel the emotions strongly enough to deliver powerful performances. Describing Linkin Park's lyrics to MTV, Bennington said, "I can't talk about this crappy thing that happened to me and expect him [Shinoda] to be able to sing it. It has to be vague enough for both of us to go, 'We can relate to it.' And we found that by writing in that way, our lyrics were hitting home with a lot of different people and a lot of different age groups."

Another characteristic of Linkin Park's lyrics is that there's no profanity. Shinoda and Bennington aren't trying to make the band sound clean-cut or nonthreatening. Instead, they see swearing as an easy way to inject intense emotions into their songs. Bennington and Shinoda prefer to challenge themselves to find other, more creative ways to describe their emotions. "We just want to be honest and not hide any emotions with vulgarity," Bennington told *Rolling Stone*.

If you tried to sum up Linkin Park with just one word, "honest" might be it. The band is honest to the emotions that drive its hard-hitting, unforgettable rock songs. The members are honest to the songwriting process: they write music that pleases them rather than trying to write music that they think will please record executives.

Chapter Four

Collision Courses

Linkin Park followed *Hybrid Theory* with three successful albums. In 2002 the band reworked its debut album with the help of Korn's Jonathan Davis, Staind's Aaron Lewis, remix specialist Kutmasta Kurt, and underground rappers such as Aceyalone and Pharoahe Monch. The result, *Reanimation*, includes innovative remixes of all the tracks off *Hybrid Theory*.

Linkin Park released its next full album of new songs, *Meteora*, in March 2003. The album debuted at number 1 on the U.S. and British charts, and at number 2 in Australia. The twelve tracks on *Meteora* see the band exploring new musical ideas. There's a ten-piece orchestra, Japanese flutes, and even a track with Shinoda on piano. The album spawned the huge hits

Bennington performs a song from the album *Collision Course* with rapper Jay-Z as part of the Music for Relief benefit in Anaheim, California, in February 2005. The album sold more than 350,000 copies in its first week.

"Somewhere I Belong" and "Numb," and earned the band another Grammy nomination—this time for the instrumental track "Session."

The band scored another number 1 debut with 2004's *Collision Course*. For an MTV show called *Ultimate Mash-Ups*, rapper Jay-Z said he was interested in working with Linkin Park. Linkin Park members jumped at the chance, and they decided to document the project with an album and DVD. The DVD follows the collaboration from Linkin Park's first meeting with Jay-Z to its studio work on mash-ups, which are remixes of songs, such as "Numb/Encore" and "Izzo/In the End" to their performance at the Roxy in Hollywood.

ON THE SIDE

You'd think that pulling off world tours and writing hit albums would be enough to keep anyone busy. But the guys of Linkin Park seem to be so full of creativity that they've taken on a number of side projects.

Bennington is working on a solo album that is set to be released in 2006. Drawing from the influence of 1990s rock and 1980s pop, including Depeche Mode and the Cure, Bennington described the music to *Rolling Stone* as "driving beats and walls of guitars." Shinoda's own side project, Fort Minor, released its first album in fall 2005. Entitled *The Rising Tied,* the album's executive producer is Jay-Z. It features guests Styles of Beyond, Common, John Legend, and the Roots member Black Thought.

Even beyond writing and recording music, Linkin Park's members have their hands full. Brad Delson writes a monthly column for the magazine *Guitar World*. Hahn has always had an interest in filmmaking. He's worked on episodes of *The X-Files*, and he's directed a number of Linkin Park's music videos, including "From the Inside" and "Numb." He's also set to make his debut as the director of a full-length feature film. The movie is a dark fantasy based on the novel *King Rat* by British author China Miéville.

The band has its own record label, Machine Shop Records. Shinoda serves as the producer for many of the label's acts, which include Simplistic and the Rosewood Fall.

Linkin Park Reaches Out

On December 26, 2004, one of the deadliest natural disasters struck without warning. An earthquake under the Indian Ocean triggered a tsunami (a giant wave) that raced toward the shores of Indonesia, Sri Lanka, India, Thailand, and Africa. The disaster left more than 200,000 dead and millions homeless.

The members of Linkin Park were deeply affected by the tragedy. They'd played sold-out shows in many of the tsunami-affected countries. Working with the American Red Cross, Linkin Park established the charity Music for Relief. The band kicked in $100,000 of its own money and encouraged its fans to donate whatever they could afford. According to the Music for Relief Web site, the organization helped push donations for the Red Cross's efforts to aid tsunami survivors to a staggering $236.2 million.

Music for Relief's efforts have continued, and a wide range of artists are on the charity's roster. Its latest effort is to bring aid to the victims of Hurricane Katrina, which devastated parts of Louisiana, Alabama, and Mississippi in 2005. The charity sponsored a series of concerts around the country shortly after the catastrophe. Ludacris, Green Day, Alicia Keys, and, not surprising, Chester Bennington were among the featured performers.

In this February 2005 photo, Bennington greets a young fan who lost her mother in the tsunami in Phuket, Thailand. When Linkin Park played in Bangkok in 2004, before the devastating natural disaster, the show was Thailand's biggest concert in more than a decade.

In 2005, the band also lent its talents to Live 8. Performing in Philadelphia, Pennsylvania, and reuniting with Jay-Z for part of its set, the band took part in a worldwide series of concerts meant to raise awareness of poverty in Africa.

Linkin Park hasn't forgotten its roots when it comes to charity. Shinoda donates all the proceeds from a pair of shoes he designed for DC Shoes to a scholarship fund for the Art Center College of Design. "It's one of the top art schools in the world, and they spend a lot of money on their students and equipment," Shinoda told MTV. "Our DJ, Mr. Hahn, went there, too, and he got fed up with how much it cost, so he ended up going somewhere else. That happens a lot there."

Other organizations the band supports include the United Way of Greater Los Angeles, the Japanese American Legacy Project, and the UCLA (University of California at Los Angeles) Foundation.

Bumps in the Road

Although they've been riding a wave of success, 2005 wasn't the easiest year for the band. Dissatisfied with Warner Music Group, the band wanted to be released from its contract. After a heated public dispute, Linkin Park agreed to stay with the label. The band accepted a five-album deal at $3 million per album.

The band's troubles have gone beyond business. After nearly nine years of marriage, Bennington and his wife, Samantha, separated in January 2005. The stress of Bennington's constant touring—even though he brought Samantha and their baby boy, Draven, along for the Meteora World Tour—likely affected the relationship.

Despite these bumps in the road, Linkin Park continues to tour. The band is also hard at work on its next album, due out in 2006. Linkin Park has always used hard times as inspiration for its music. It won't be surprising if the band uses the recent turbulent events to make the next album its best yet.

Timeline

1996 Mike Shinoda, Brad Delson, Dave "Phoenix" Farrell, Rob Bourdon, and Joseph Hahn form Xero. Chester Bennington meets and marries Samantha.

1997 Bennington auditions for and joins Xero. The band changes its name to Hybrid Theory.

1999 The band releases the Hybrid Theory EP.

2000 Hybrid Theory signs a record deal with the Warner Music Group. The band changes its name to Linkin Park. *Hybrid Theory* is released on October 24.

2001 The Recording Industry Association of America certifies *Hybrid Theory* platinum (a designation for albums that sell at least 1 million copies) on January 1. Bennington and Samantha have a baby, Draven.

2002 Linkin Park receives three Grammy nominations and wins a Grammy for the Best Hard Rock Performance.

2003 *Meteora* is released.

2004 Linkin Park collaborates with Jay-Z for the album *Collision Course*. Linkin Park starts a charity called Music for Relief after a devastating tsunami strikes several countries in Asia.

2005 Linkin Park plays the Live 8 concert in Philadelphia, Pennsylvania.

Discography

2000 *Hybrid Theory*

2003 *Meteora*

Remixes and live albums

2002 *Reanimation*

2003 *Live in Texas*

2004 *Collision Course*

Soundtracks

2000 *Dracula 2000, Little Nicky*

2001 *Valentine*

2002 *Queen of the Damned*

2003 *The Matrix Reloaded*

Other limited-edition albums are available through the band's official Web site and fan club (http://linkinpark.com).

DVDs

Linkin Park: Frat Party at the Pankake Festival. WEA Corp./ Warner Brothers, 2001.

Linkin Park: Unauthorized. Music Video Distributors, 2002.

Linkin Park: Live in Texas. WEA Corp., 2003.

Linkin Park: Breaking the Habit. WEA Corp., 2004.

Collision Course. WEA Corp., 2004.

Glossary

demo A recording that a band uses to book shows and send to record labels.

genre A style within music, film, writing, or other forms of art.

grunge A style of music that originated in the Seattle, Washington, music scene and became popular during the late 1980s and early 1990s. The grunge sound was heavily influenced by punk rock.

hybrid A combination of two or more things. For example, Linkin Park's music is a hybrid of musical genres including rock, rap, and heavy metal.

mash-up A remix that combines the lyrics of one popular song with the music of another.

methamphetamine A very dangerous and addictive family of illegal drugs. "Crystal meth" is a common street name.

nü-metal A style of heavy rock music that emerged in the mid- to late 1990s. It often features drumming and vocals that are influenced by rap and hip-hop.

record label A company that pays musicians to record albums and helps promote the albums.

showcase A special performance for representatives from a record label.

For More Information

Linkin Park
c/o Warner Bros. Records
P.O. Box 6868
Burbank, CA 91510
(818) 846-9090
Web site: http://www.
    linkinpark.com

MTV Networks
1515 Broadway
New York, NY 10036
(212) 258-8000
Web site: http://www.mtv.com/
    bands/az/linkin_park/
    artist.jhtml

Rolling Stone
1290 Avenue of the Americas
New York, NY 10104-0298
(212) 484-1616
Web site: http://www.
    rollingstone.com/artists/
    linkinpark

Web Sites

Due to the changing nature of Internet links, the Rosen Publishing Group, Inc., has developed an online list of Web sites related to the subject of this book. This site is updated regularly. Please use this link to access the list:

http://www.rosenlinks.com/
cmtm/lipa

For Further Reading

Baltin, Steve, Greg Watermann, and David Fricke. *From the Inside: Linkin Park's* Meteora. Agoura Hills, CA: Bradson Press, 2004.

Bukszpan, Daniel. *The Encyclopedia of Heavy Metal*. New York, NY: Barnes and Noble, 2003.

Graham, Ben. *Linkin Park: The Unauthorised Biography in Words & Pictures*. London, England: Chrome Dreams, 2001.

McIver, Joel. *Nu-Metal: The Next Generation of Rock and Punk*. London, England: Omnibus Press, 2002.

Porter, Dick. *Rapcore: The Nu-Metal Rap Fusion*. London, England: Plexus Publishing, 2003.

Bibliography

Cummer, Chris. "Linkin Park." Native Instruments. Retrieved August 16, 2005 (http://www.nativeinstruments.de/index.php?id=linkinpark_us&flash=0).

DiMartino, Dave. "Parkin' with Linkin Park." Yahoo! Music. October 12, 2003. Retrieved August 16, 2005 (http://music.yahoo.com/read/interview/12060975).

Eliscu, Jenny. "Linkin Park." *Rolling Stone*, January 2001.

Graff, Gary. "Local Heroes." *Guitar World*, December 2000.

Grogan, Siobhan. "'We Wouldn't Sign You for a Million Dollars.'" *Guardian*. March 21, 2003.

Montgomery, James, and Vanessa Wolf. "Two New Projects Let Fans Walk a Mile in Linkin Park's Shoes." MTV. November 18, 2004. Retrieved August 19, 2005 (http://www.mtv.com/news/articles/1493525/20041108/linkin_park.jhtml).

Moss, Corey, and Peter Wilkinson. "Linkin Park: In the Beginning." MTV. March 2002. Retrieved August 16, 2005 (http://www.mtv.com/bands/l/linkin_park/news_feature_mar_02/index.jhtml).

Sindell, Joshua. "Interview with Chester Bennington." *Kerrang!* August 2, 2003. Retrieved August 28, 2005 (http://www.pushmeaway.com/kerrangchesint03.html).

Index

About the Author

Greg Saulmon is a writer and rock guitarist living in Easthampton, Massachusetts. His bands have performed in New York City, Boston, Atlanta, Chicago, and Nashville.

Photo Credits

Designer: Gene Mollica; **Editor:** Jun Lim
Photo Researcher: Gene Mollica